RUMI

THE RUMI CARD BOOK

THE RUMI

ERYK

RUMI: THE CARD AND BOOK PACK
Meditation, Inspiration, Self-Discovery
CREATED BY
ERYK HANUT AND MICHELE WETHERBEE

CARD BOOK

HANUT

JOURNEY EDITIONS
BOSTON · RUTLAND, VERMONT · TOKYO

First published in 2000 by Journey Editions, an imprint of Tuttle Publishing, with editorial offices at 153 Milk Street, Boston, Massachusetts 02109.

Copyright © 2000 Eryk Hanut

Library of Congress Cataloging-in-Publication Data

Hanut, Eryk
    Rumi : the card and book pack : meditation, inspiration, self-
  discovery. The rumi card book / by Eryk Hanut. The rumi card and
  book pack / created by Eryk Hanut and Michele Wetherbee. -- 1st ed.
      p. cm.
  Includes bibliographical references.
  ISBN 1-885203-95-0 (hardcover)
  1. Divination cards. 2. Self-actualization (Psychology)-
  -Miscellanea. 3. Jalal al-Din Rumi, Maulana, 1207–1273.
  I. Wetherbee, Michele. II. Title.
  BF1778.5.H36 2000
  133.3'242--dc21   99-40397
                                          CIP

Distributed by

USA
Tuttle Publishing
Distribution Center
Airport Industrial Park
364 Innovation Drive
North Clarendon, VT 05759-9436
Tel: (802) 773-8930
Tel: (800) 526-2778

Canada
Raincoast Books
8680 Cambie Street
Vancouver, British Columbia
V6P 6M9
Tel: (604) 323-7100
Fax: (604) 323-2600

Japan
Tuttle Publishing
RK Building, 2nd Floor
2-13-10 Shimo-Meguro, Meguro-Ku
Tokyo 153 0064
Tel: (03) 5437-0171
Fax: (03) 5437-0755

Southeast Asia
Berkeley Books Pte Ltd
5 Little Road #08-01
Singapore 536983
Tel: (65) 280-1330
Fax: (65) 280-6290

First edition
06 05 04 03 02 01 00   10 9 8 7 6 5 4 3 2 1

Package and design were created by Michele Wetherbee.
Illustrations © Stefan Gutermuth are based on traditional Islamic art.
Printed in China

for Mara Singer,
My beloved sister, best buddy, and favorite sibyl.

ACKNOWLEDGMENTS

I would like to thank Andrew Harvey for his love, patience, his extraordinary passion and knowledge of Sufism, and his unmatched skills with the English language.

My deep gratitude to Tom Grady, my friend and agent at the Thomas Grady Agency, for his kindness, belief in my work, stamina, and constant encouragement.

Jan Johnson at Tuttle was and is the kindest and most helpful of editors. Her patience and advice during the making of this deck were appreciated in a way that no words could ever express.

I want to thank Michele Wetherbee for the beauty of her talent, her humor, and for believing in this project.

Rumi said, "Giving thanks for the power to act increases your power." I thank God for having surrounded me all my life with so many creative, talented, and sometimes wild and crazy people right from the beginning. Some of you have left this Earth but not my heart. Many of you are around me. I give thanks to and for: Lauren Artress, Rebecca Ghittino, Nathalie Burton, Teresa A. Bright, Barbara, Fran Bull, Bridget Bell, Mollie Corcoran, Caroline and Françoise Bouteraon, Harriet Fields, Sara Foster, Edwige Feuillere, Jacques and Annette Hanut, John and Lisa Hunt, Barbara Hartford, Sharon Kehoe, Robert Snyder, Helen McDermott, Ariane, Carl, and Nora Genevrois, Susan and Lance Morrow,

Barbara Groth, Mary and Axel Grabowsky, Kathleen Granby, Traci Cochran, Rose Solari, Karine, Muriel, and Louise Deschoenmakers, Dorothy Walters, Renee Saint Cyr, Henry and Leila Luce, Karen Kellejian, Joey Singer, Jean-Louis Hanut, Maria Todisco, Gloria Vanderbilt, Sylvie Vartan, Peggy Wright, Kristina Grace, Jean-Yves Bolen, Mary Grady, Gustavine Van Weynendaele, Betty Harvey, Purrball and Oscar Van Weynendaele.

TABLE OF CONTENTS

Wisdom is like the rain. Its source is limitless, but it comes down according to the season.

Grocers put sugar in a bag; their supply of sugar, however, is not limited to what's in the bag. When you come to a grocer, he has an abundant supply of sugar. But he sees how much money you have brought with you and measures out the sugar accordingly.

Your money on the Path of God is courage and faith, and you will be taught according to your courage and faith.

—Rumi.

Come, come, whoever you are—
wanderer, worshiper, lover of leaving—
what does it matter?
Ours is not a caravan of despair.
Come, even if you have broken your vow
a hundred times—
come, come again, come.

—Rumi

A QUARREL ABOUT GRAPES

A man gave a coin to four different people. One of them, a Persian, said, "I want to buy some anghur with that!" The second man was an Arab and he said, "I want inab not anghur, you worthless fool!" The third was a Turk and he said, "This is my money and I don't want inab. I want uzum!" The fourth, a Greek, shouted, "Shut up all of you! I want israfi!"

In their madness, the four started to argue and hit each other because they didn't know the hidden meaning of names. They battered each other with their fists because they were empty of true knowledge and filled with ignorance.

If an authentic mystic master, proficient in many languages, had been there, they would have been pacified. He would have said, "I can give you everything you want with this one coin; if you give me your heart sincerely and without dissimulation, this coin will accomplish all you want. Your one coin will become four; four enemies will become one heart. All you say only produces struggle and separation; what I tell you brings harmony. So be quiet now, so I can talk for you."

—Rumi, in the Mathnawi

PART I

WHO IS THIS RUMI?

PROLOGUE

"You don't believe me. You think I am crazy; but he will come."

I looked at the old man, impeccably dressed, all in white and with gold-rimmed spectacles, a Turkish Cesar Romero. He looked unconvincing, and unconvinced I said, "Of course I believe you."

It was at the end of the summer of 1993. I was accompanying Andrew Harvey on one of his returns to South India and we had decided, on our way, to stop in Istanbul. For Andrew, it was Turkey, the homeland of Rumi. For me, it was a discovery, a way of trying to walk in the footsteps of Pierre Loti, a French novelist at the end of the nineteenth century and an old childhood obsession of mine. The city was a radiant slap in the face for me. It is said that the Emperor Justinian, entering the new Church of Haghia Sophia that he had commissioned, exclaimed "Oh Solomon, I have surpassed thee."

I wanted to see everything: the Blue Mosque, the Bridge over the Bosphorus where Occident becomes Orient, the covered markets with their hundreds of carpet stalls, the diamond-studded swords of the Sultans in the Topkapi.

One evening, two days before we were due to leave for India, we were having dinner in a small restaurant of a seedy quarter overlooking an eruption of minarets. It was the kind of place where cocks fight between tables and you don't know if fried spinach,

"Rosa Persica Essence," or dog poop will be the next smell to strike your nostrils. There we encountered that old man dressed in white, seated among the chess players, reading an old leather-bound book. He got up and strode to our table as if responding to a silent invitation and told us that he was reading Rumi.

"Rumi?" I said, and the eyes of the old man in white seemed to mist over.

"Yes," he said softly in clear English with only a slight Turkish accent. "I've been every evening in this restaurant for the last ten months, reading the Master and waiting for my friend."

I looked around and wondered how he had kept so immaculate coming here every evening for ten months.

He went on: "My best friend disappeared ten months ago; nobody knows where he is; but I know that he will come here soon. He will come back and we will meet in this restaurant." "How do you know?" I asked a little testily. He pointed to his old book, "All the answers are here; Rumi knew everything; his words told me to come here and wait."

Then, as calmly and elegantly as he had come, he walked back to his table to finish his glass of tea and then left.

The waiter—a young man with missing teeth—explained in his one-third English, one-third French, and one-third Bulgarian that the old man was deranged. To prove it, he drilled his finger in his right temple. Then, while bringing tea, he tried to sell us "coins from Justinian's time." They were probably made in Taiwan.

On the last day of our stay in Istanbul, inspired by a strange curiosity, we went back to the seedy restaurant (whose honey-soaked pastries, it must be said, were sublime). There, smiling ecstatically, the old man was sitting, holding hands with a plump older man in a suit with large lapels and big thick gold glasses. He bore a resemblance to King Farouk, whom I had seen on the old stamps of my sister's collection. "See," the old man almost shouted. "See, he came." Then looking at me with a tinge of irony, a hand on his old leathered book, he whispered, "Everything true is in it; you simply have to ask the Master; what did I tell you?" And he quoted:

Love makes the seas boil like a pot
And rubbles the mountains to sand
And splits the heavens into fragments
And makes tremble the entire earth.

AND IT CAME TO BE

A year later, I found myself in a whirlwind of anxiety. We had moved from Paris to California, and the state of my non-existent career was a constant worry. My health too had declined dangerously. I felt helpless, as if I were drowning and unable to seek any spiritual guidance.

One morning, Andrew Harvey advised me to pick a sentence from Rumi's work at random and to use it as guidance for the day. I remembered that Gregory the Great used this method of "divination" with the Bible. I knew also that in India, the Bhagavad Gita can be consulted like this. But Gregory the Great had died long ago; and I was not Indian. I thought momentarily about the old man in Istanbul. Then, again, who was he? Had he really been telling the truth? Was the Farouk look-alike really the friend he had been waiting for?

But I was desperate. I finally opened the *Mathnawi* of Rumi, and, as I had been advised, closed my eyes and picked a sentence. When I opened my eyes, I read "Gold becomes constantly more and more beautiful from the blow the jeweler inflicts on it." Brilliant, I thought ironically, "Just what I need to hear!" Totally unimpressed, I shut the book and went on cursing my life and the world for the rest of the day.

The next morning, my dear friend Sara Foster, who lives in Mississippi, sent me a card. Sara is a beautiful artist, and her watercolors always have the freshness of the first dawn of time. Under a rich red rose she had painted for me was written, in calligraphy, "Gold becomes constantly more and more beautiful from the blows the jeweler inflicts on it."

The coincidence shook me.

But it still did not occur to me that Heaven could try to communicate with a mind as smart as mine.

The following afternoon, I was walking down Haight Street to meet some friends when I came across Larry. Larry was a homeless man, with a face like an Old Testament prophet's and sweet ice-blue eyes. Sometimes he would shake all over from delirium tremens. At others, he would claim he had won the Pulitzer Prize. That morning he asked me, "So, how are you?" I replied, "Oh, not great." Larry looked at me ceremoniously and said, "Gold becomes more and more beautiful from the blows the jeweler inflicts on it." Startled, I asked him where he had found the quote from Rumi. He smiled mysteriously. "I have my ways," he said, "I am not an ignoramus, you know."

I walked into Booksmith and found a volume of Rumi's poetry. I concentrated, closed my eyes, and opened the book at "With this pain, you are digging a path for yourself to God."

Suddenly, tears came to my eyes; I felt so weak I had to sit down. I realized that what the strange old man had told me in Istanbul was not an exotic fable but a simple—and astounding—truth. And I remembered something he had said that I had forgotten,

"The whole universe is a book and speaks to us in each event. And the whole universe is in Rumi."

Out of these linked experiences came the idea of creating the deck you have in your hands, a deck of cards that would make available to anyone who wanted it—and as clearly and directly as possible—the life, wisdom, and heart-guidance of Rumi.

I want everyone who sees these cards to experience what I did: Rumi's timeless voice speaking to me, and to the heart of what I was suffering, words of strengthening truth. As Rumi wrote, "Do not go into the direction of despair; I tell you, Suns exist." And: "How long will you move backward? Come forward; do not stay in unbelief. Come dancing to divine knowledge."

This Rumi deck represents the essence of Rumi's mystical wisdom and provides a way of helping everyone find answers to the questions of their lives—from the most mundane worries that can still, as we all know, be a source of suffering and anxiety—to those profound questions about the nature of life and the meaning of our destiny that obsess us all at times, whether we want them to or not. What I hope this Rumi deck offers everyone is a way to "come dancing to divine knowledge."

Rumi himself loved to help all beings at whatever stage and in whatever difficulties they found themselves. He was a famously tender and tolerant man who loved to see people happy and at peace with their lives and with God. He was also a worker of miracles and a great healer, both of soul and body.

THE GUIDES SURROUND US

What I hope we have created in this book and card deck is an instrument through which Rumi can continue in our time his eternal work of healing instructions and spiritual help and guidance in a way that is accessible, easy to use, and that encourages us to develop our own powers of receptivity and mystical intuition and to join him in a ceaseless living dialogue of Love beyond space and time. Rumi knew that such an external dialogue was possible between these lovers of the beloved. As he said in his *Table-Talk*:

> *When our guides and those who are cherished by us leave and disappear, they are not annihilated. They are like stars that vanish into the light of the Sun of Reality. They exist by their essence and are made invisible by their attributes. This subject has no end. If all the seas of the world were ink, and all the trees of all the forests were pens, and all the atoms of the air were scribes, still they could not describe the unions and reunions of pure and divine souls and their reciprocal loves.*

Rumi's first biographer, Aflaki, wrote about a half-century after his death:

> *Sultan Valad, our Master's son, recounted: "One day I said to my father, 'The friends claim that when they do not see you it causes them pain and their inner joy disappears.' My father replied, 'Whoever does not*

feel joyful in my absence does not really know me;
the one who really knows me feels happy even with-
out me; he will be suffused with me, with the thought
of me, with my thought.' He added, 'Every time, my
son, that you find yourself in a state of mystic sweet-
ness know that this state is me in you.'" Sultan Valad
added, "This is why my father used to say, 'When
you look for me, look in the district of joy: We are
the inhabitants of the world of joy.'"

—*From Aflaki:* Biography of Rumi

Aflaki also tells the story of one day when some scholars of Konya got into an argument about their different views on grammar, philosophy, astronomy, and religion. After hours of fruitless discussion, they agreed to write down the most difficult questions and to submit them to the Master Rumi.

They found him reading on the side of the road that goes to the Sultan's palace. Immediately, and without looking at what was written on the sheets of paper, Rumi asked for a bottle of ink and a feather and, unhesitatingly, wrote down the most accurate answers to each question. The answers were delivered to the Tribunal of the wise men, who were amazed at their accuracy.

The scholars went in procession to thank Rumi, who declared: "This great grace streams from Heaven, and not from the terrestrial world. It comes from joy and from the Stars, and not from the strength of any of our arms."

All the great mystical traditions agree that, as you wake up slowly to your divine identity, you are graced with certain powers. These can include psychic abilities such as the gift of divining the future.

Many mystics from all traditions have experienced this and used their powers to help others in their difficulties and to avoid or transcend the dangers of life. These include, of course, millions of so-called "ordinary people" like you and me, whom the world may never hear of but who are what Jesus called "The salt of the Earth."

From the earliest shamans to Jesus and Ramakrishna, from Francis of Assisi to Pope John XXIII, from the first wise women to the Druids and Wiccan practitioners, and all of those hundreds of thousands today who are waking to their Goddess-given powers, the chosen ones who are able to lift the veil between the two worlds are innumerable. Rumi said, "At every moment, Love's voice talks to us from left and from right, all we have to do is to know how to listen."

Aflaki tells us that, as with the Poverello of Assisi, trees and animals would bow with reverence when the Master was passing by. "Sages are the mirrors of God's eternal wisdom," Rumi wrote. And it is clear that those who are open can hear God's voice everywhere.

Astonishing scientific research such as that cited in the work of Larry Dossey proves the power of prayer to heal the body. Recent discoveries in astrophysics reveal the interdependence of all atomic particles. The pioneer-gardeners of Findhorn—a group of ostensibly "ordinary" people who chose, in the 1960s, to grow fruits and vegetables in the north of Scotland, were guided and instructed directly by Spirits of Nature called "Devas." Their experiments yielded the most astonishing results—oversize melons in a soil that could barely sustain heather and immense tomatoes and lettuces on a land that for centuries had supported rocks and thistles—only confirming what mystics always knew: that everything is interconnected in the Great Unity.

In one of his Odes, Rumi gives us this teaching:

From the moment you came into this world,
A ladder was placed in front of you,
That you might transcend it.
From earth, you became plant,
From plant, you became animal,
Afterwards, you became a human being
Endowed with knowledge, intellect and faith.

Behold the body, born of dust,
How perfect it has become.
Why should you fear its end?
Where were you ever made less by dying?
When you pass beyond this human form
No doubt you will become an angel
And soar through the Heavens,
But don't stop there, even heavenly bodies grow old.
Pass again from the heavenly realm and

Plunge, plunge into the vast ocean of consciousness,
Let the drop of water that is you
Become a hundred mighty seas.

But do not think that the drop alone
Becomes the ocean.
The ocean too becomes the drop.

Not only then are all things and events connected, but all things and events are part of an "endless" evolution, of a process that is destined to take us, if we allow it, to as yet unimaginable heights of vision and illumination and fusion with God. To help us on this vast and glorious journey, the Divine has insured that signs, encouragement, and omens dance all around us. All we need to do is to develop our God-given ability to read them. Whether you call this "Universal Wisdom," "Instinct," "Premonition," or "Guardian Angel" is not important. What matters is to have faith in your Divine identity and in your right to constant direct guidance. As Rumi said so beautifully, "Believe in love's infinite journey, for it is your own, for you are love."

May this deck, created from the inspiration of one of the World's greatest mystics, help you discover within yourself unseen treasures of Love, Endurance, and Wisdom.

Rumi wrote: "The intellect says: 'The six directions are limits: There is no way out.' Love says: 'There is a way. I have traveled it thousands of times.'"

May this deck open up love's way to all those who sincerely wish to take it in the middle of the world's difficulty and confusion! May it awaken all beings to the humility, passion, and radiant inspired intelligence of the way of love—that "way" that can guide us all into our deeper joy and fullest wisdom!

THE LIFE OF RUMI

> Sometimes, very rarely, there appear on earth beings whose grandeur and sweetness reveal a wholly new human possibility, a creation that has still not been revealed and which it is all our duties to discover, celebrate, and embody.
>
> —Pierre Teilhard de Chardin

I believe Rumi is such a being. To know something of his life is to begin to celebrate and embody our own possibility.

Rumi, the greatest mystic of Islam—and perhaps of the world—was born in Balkh (now Afghanistan) on September 30, 1207. He died in Konya (Turkey) in his sixty-seventh year on December 17, 1273, the night of the "marriage" between Rumi's soul and God.

As a record of his extraordinary life, lived on the wildest and grandest heights of the Spirit, Rumi left behind a mystical epic in six immense volumes, the *Mathnawi*, 3,500 odes to his beloved spiritual mentor Shams of Tabriz, 2,000 quatrains, a book of table talk, and several volumes of letters. The Mevlevi order that he founded and that was continued by his son, Sultan Walad, endured persecution and oppression in many eras to spread Rumi's vision all over Africa and Asia and, eventually, everywhere in the world.

In the last twenty years, through the pioneering translations of Coleman Barks, Robert Bly, Andrew Harvey, and others, Rumi has become, as Bill Moyers pointed out in his recent television series on poetry, "the most popular poet in America," read by seekers of all kinds and persuasions and creeds. In a recent CD made by Deepak Chopra, Rumi's poems were read by Demi Moore, KD Lang, and Madonna, among others. A new hour-long video about Rumi ("Rumi: Poet of the Heart"), featuring Coleman Barks, Robert Bly, and Huston Smith, and narrated by Debra Winger, has just been released. For hundreds of thousands of seekers of all religions and all paths, Rumi's work has become a way of connecting directly to the Divine within each of us beyond the constrictions of religion or dogma.

Rumi himself remained a strict and observant Muslim all of his life. But, as a Sufi member of the broad-minded and open-souled mystical tradition of Islam, Rumi honored all paths that led to union with the Divine, and he exemplified, both in his work and in his life, an extreme tolerance for all approaches to God.

There are a myriad different ways to search, but the object is always the same. Don't you see that the roads are different? One comes from Byzantium, another from Syria, still others wind through land or across the seas. The roads are different; the goal is one. Generations have passed and this is a new generation. The moon is always the same, only the water changes. The water in the stream may have changed a million times. The reflection of the moon and stars are the same.

With such an all-embracing vision, it is not surprising that Rumi has become, for many Americans, their favorite spiritual friend—brother and guide to the deep mysteries of Divine Love, whatever path they may be on.

What Rumi in his life and work combined, at the highest level and with the greatest possible intensity, was the intellect of a Plato, the vision and soul-force of a Christ and a Buddha, and the exquisite, extraordinary literary genius of a Shakespeare. This fusion of the highest spirituality with the most complete artistic gifts gives Rumi a unique position in the history of the world—and a unique power as a prophet and initiator into the sacred.

In one of his last short poems to his spiritual beloved, Shams, Rumi wrote:

Those tender words we said to one another
are stored in the secret heart of heaven
one day, like the rain, they will fall and spread
and their mystery will grow green over the world.

The time has clearly arrived for this "Greening" of the world's heart and mind by the mystery of Rumi's love for the divine. What might be called "The Return of Rumi" to the consciousness of the planet is, many believe, no coincidence. Rumi's visionary teachings are returning to empower as many people as can open to them with the truths of sacred love and adoration of the Creator and creation at a moment when we all need to be empowered by their holy passion if the planet and nature is to be preserved.

Rumi is not only perhaps the world's greatest mystic but also an essential and marvelously non-dogmatic guide to the new planetary spiritual renaissance that is struggling to be born in the ruins of all of our old ways of thinking and feeling. He speaks to us out of the depths of our own sacred truth, and what he says has the transforming eloquence of our own innermost truth.

Define and narrow me, you starve yourself of yourself
Nail me down in a box of cold words,
That box is your coffin.
I do not know who I am.
I am in astounded lucid confusion.
I am not a Christian, not a Jew, not a Zoroastrian,
I am not even a Muslim...
I am the life of life.
I am that cat, this stone, no one...
I see and know all times and worlds
As one, one, always one.
What do I have
To do to get you to admit who is speaking?
Admit it and change everything!
This is your own voice echoing off the walls of God.

If we dare to accept Rumi's incandescent challenge and admit that the voice singing through him of divine love and divine identity is, in fact, our *own* voice, and the secret voice of every human soul in communion with God, then amazing visions and powers will be granted us, and the real new age will begin to be born—the age of a free, creative divinely inspired and guided humanity, liberated at last from all visions of limitation and all traditions of mind-slavery.

It was Rumi's extraordinary and prophetic greatness that he lived and embodied the love and creativity and freedom of this new age of humanity seven hundred years before its birth on a massive world-wide scale became at last possible. Will we be loving and wild and adventurous and trusting enough to follow him—and those like him—into the glories and dangers of new birth?

On our answer may well depend the future. May the divine beloved give us, then, Rumi's vision and bravery! And may this deck be, in its own way, one of the helpful midwives of the new birth.

Rumi was born in Balkh, a city famous for its beauty, in Khorassan (now Afghanistan) on September 30, 1207 AD. His real name was Jalal-ad-Din. "Rumi" comes from "Rum," the region of Anatolia in Turkey in which he later lived. His family was a highly distinguished one of jurists and religious scholars who traced their lineage back to Abu Bakr, one of the companions of the Prophet Muhammed and the first Caliph after his death.

His father, Baha-ud-din-Valad (whom Rumi revered), was a famous theologian, Sufi master, and visionary, called by his contemporaries "The Sultan of Scholars." He was already sixty when Rumi was born and is said to have treated his son with great tenderness. What little survives of his writings shows him to have been a passionate and exalted mystic, like his son.

The epoch Rumi was born into was one like ours, of chaotic violence and turmoil. The Ottoman Empire was menaced from within and without. From within, it was menaced by political decadence and corruption, and from without, by Christian invaders from the West and the Mongol armies of Genghis Khan from the East. Rumi's life was seared by this turmoil early on. At the age of 12, in 1219, he was forced to flee Balkh with his father, who was being attacked by religious enemies and who foresaw the destruction of the city by Genghis Khan that occurred a year later.

For a decade, Rumi wandered with his family all over Asia Minor and Arabia. They are said to have made a pilgrimage to Mecca and to have stopped on the way at Nishapur, in central Iran, where the young Rumi met the great Persian Sufi poet Attar, author of "The Conference of the Birds," and who offered him a copy of another of his mystical masterpieces, *The Book of Secrets*.

Attar predicted of him, "This boy will open a gate in the heart of love and throw a flame into the heart of all mystic lovers."

In later years, Rumi would honor Attar at every opportunity and say of him, "Attar has traveled through all the seven cities of love while I still live on the corner of a narrow street."

Later in his travels, Rumi went to Damascus in Syria, where he met the old Ibn Arabi, the greatest Sufi metaphysician of his age. The legend goes that when Ibn Arabi saw Rumi walking behind his father, he exclaimed, "Glory be to God, an ocean is walking behind a lake!"

At eighteen, Rumi married Gauher-Kathoun, the beautiful daughter of Hodja Charif-Od, a grandee of Samarkhand, and rapidly fathered two sons with her–Sultan Valad and Ala-od-Din-Tchelebi. Sultan Valad would grow up especially close to his father, collected and condensed his teachings in his own works in *The Secret Word* and *Master and Disciple*, and continued his father's order.

After stays in Laranda and Arzanian in Armenia, Rumi's father was invited, in 1229, by Ala-Ud-Din Kaykobad, the Sultan of Konya in central Turkey, to go and live there. The Sultan built a college especially for Rumi's father, who taught there to great acclaim until his death two years later at the age of 84. Immediately after the death of his beloved father, Rumi was chosen to be his successor. Already his brilliance, charisma, and spiritual depth had made him famous. He was only twenty-four years old.

Rumi's first spiritual teacher is said to have been an old disciple of his father named Muhaqiq Tirmidhi.

Rumi studied with him for nine years, during which he traveled to Damascus, where he met again the great mystic Ibn Arabi, and may well have been instructed by him into the deeper intellectual and spiritual aspects of Sufi philosophy.

After seven years of teaching and studying in Syria, Rumi returned to Konya and soon became a famous teacher of jurisprudence and canonical law. He was also, by this time, a spiritual director who soon collected a vast following. By 1244, wrote his son, Sultan Valad, in *The Secret Word*, Rumi had "ten thousand disciples."

Everything seemed golden for the young Rumi, but he was far from being the great sage he would become. As he wrote himself much later, "I was raw, and then I was cooked, and then, I was consumed." What cooked and consumed him was his meeting with Shams of Tabriz. The total transformation and alchemy that made him the Rumi we think we know today bloomed from this encounter.

Of Shams of Tabriz Rumi was to write:

I have seen the king with a face of glory,
He who is the eye and the sun of heaven,
He who is the companion and healer of all beings,
He who is the soul and the universe that births souls.

Shams of Tabriz, then in his sixties, was a strange, wild man, a hermit and a wanderer. His ferocious, often scornful temperament had made him many enemies. Shams was what Sufi mystics call an "Abdal," a hidden saint. As Sultan Valad wrote of him, "Many great saints did not find Shams of Tabriz although they looked and looked. It was God's jealousy that hid him far from the imagination and thought of others."

The legend goes that Shams prayed for years to meet someone who would be able to stand his intensity and receive the full transmission of everything he had learned and of all that Love had given him.

One day, God spoke to him and asked him what he would give in exchange. Shams offered him his life. Then God told him to go to Konya, where he would meet the mystic beloved destined for him, Jalal-ad-Din, the son of Baha-ud-Din of Balkh.

Directed by this vision, Shams arrived in Konya at sunset on November 29, 1244. There, he rented a miserable room near the market square and retreated for days, fasting, praying, and waiting.

As to how Shams and Rumi actually met, no one is really sure. The loveliest of all the many versions is that Shams accosted Rumi as he was riding a donkey through the square of Konya, followed by a horde of disciples. Abruptly, the wild dervish appeared from nowhere and challenged him: "Who was the greatest of all prophets, Bayazid or Muhammad?" Rumi answered that that was a bizarre question, considering that Muhammad was beyond all prophets.

Shams replied, "So, in this case, what did Muhammad mean when he told God, 'I didn't know You as I should have,' while Bayazid said, 'Glory to me! How exalted is my dignity!'"

At these words, Rumi fainted and fell off his donkey. When he came to in the dust, he staggered up, grabbed Shams by the hand and led him to a room of his college, where they locked themselves away from the world for 40 days. What Shams had given Rumi as he spoke the words of the great Sufi mystic Bayazid was a direct initiation into the glory of his—and everyone's—divine identity. This initiation destroyed what Rumi thought he knew, and new knowledge would now flower in revelation after revelation.

Another version of the meeting is that Shams strode into Rumi's class one day and, pointing to a pile of books on the floor, cried out, "You don't know anything about what's written in these books." At these words, the volumes burst into flame. Rumi shouted, "What is happening?" Shams replied icily, "You don't know," and swept out. Rumi then, it is said, left his family and followed after him.

Another version of the meeting between Shams and Rumi, by the chronicler Djami, tells us that Rumi was sitting by a fountain and had put down some books by his side. Shams walked by and asked, "What are these?" Rumi is said to have answered, "These are words; why on earth should you bother about them? "Shams then seized the books and threw them into the water. Rumi shouted, "How dare you! In some of these books were manuscripts of my father you can't find anywhere else!" Shams then plunged his hand into the water and took the books out one by one and, miraculously, none of them were wet. Rumi asked,

"What is your secret?" Shams answered, "Dhawq (Desire for God) and Hal (spiritual state)! Why on earth should you bother about them?" Bemused and humbled, Rumi embraced him and the two men went into seclusion.

In a fourth version of their meeting, Shams is said to have accosted Rumi in the street and asked him, "What is the goal of spiritual striving and mortification or the repetition of prayers?" Rumi replied, "To understand the tradition and the customs of religious law." Shams cried out, "All that is external." Rumi asked him, "What is the goal then?" Shams replied, "True knowledge consists in passing from the unknown to the known." Shams then quoted two lines from an ode by the great Persian mystic Sanal: "If knowledge does not lift you from your self, it would be better for you to stay ignorant."

Whatever version you accept—and each of them contains something of the essential truth of their relationship—the meeting between Shams and Rumi led to Rumi's extreme transformation. For the next sixteen months, Rumi would be "cooked" by the fiery wisdom and passion of his new mentor. In Rumi, Shams would finally meet the being to whom he could transmit his essence. He was the beloved who could bear the fury and splendor of his love, the radiant burden of the sublime exchange of hearts and souls.

Rumi's son, Sultan Valad, wrote:

Since my father was closest of all beings through purity and sincerity to God, God consented that

Shams could manifest to him and that this manifestation should be for him alone. My father desired no other person but Shams. He never abandoned in his heart the love of the Eternal. Even if someone else had come, he could not have deserved the gift of his love. It was my father alone who was worthy of such a vision, after so long a wait, he saw the face of Shams and the secrets became for him clear as day light. He saw what cannot be seen and heard what cannot be heard and received what no one has ever received from anyone else. He fell in love with Shams and was annihilated.

What really happened between the two men during the sixteen months that followed could only be guessed at from what Rumi wrote about it:

Seizing my life in your hands,
You thrashed it clean
On the savage rocks of eternal mind.
How its colors bled, until they grew white!
You smile and sit back: I dry in your sun.

We are like the night, earth's Shadow.
He is the sun: He splits open the night
With a sword soaked in dawn.

I have given up existence, why go on staggering
Under the burden of this mountain?
Since the wolf is my shepherd, why put up with
The pretensions of the Shepherd?
Blessed is the place you are, and glorious

To the eye of the heart.
Each atom, by your grace, is a universe,
Each drop of water a soul.
From your beauty ablaze like the Sun,.
From the curls of your hair,
My heart has become ecstatic.

In another piece, Rumi wrote:

SINCE YOU ARE I, YOU WHO ARE MYSELF

Once a man came and knocked at the door of his
friend.
"Who are you?" asked his friend. "It is I," he replied.
The friend said, "Go away! This isn't the time to enter!
There's no place at a table like mine for the one
Who's not been cooked in the fire of true gnosis."
Apart from the fire of absence and separation
What'll cook the raw or free the uncooked from
fraud?
The poor man went away and for a whole year of
travel and absence
He was burnt utterly by the flames of separation.
His heart burned until it was consumed; he came again
To the door of his friend and knocked at the door
With a hundred signs of the utmost fear and reverence,
Terrified a wrong word should escape his lips.
From within, his friend called out, "Who's at the
door?"
He replied, "It is you who are at the door, o charmer
of hearts!"

"Since you are I," the friend said, "O you who are myself,

Enter; there's no place in my house for two I's."

In *The Way of Passion*, Andrew Harvey described the first year of the meeting between Shams and Rumi in the following way: "A massive transformation took place, a transmission from Sham's heart to Rumi's heart. The terrifying speed, wildness, violence and ferocity of Rumi's transformation were essential. Shams knew he had very little time and that Rumi had to be utterly and completely remade for the revelation he was destined to transmit to be potent in him." From the moment Shams met Rumi, he knew his fate was sealed. He would die soon. Everything he knew and was had to be transmitted to Rumi extremely fast and intensely.

Rumi's disciples became increasingly jealous of Sham's influence on their teacher; Shams was forced to flee back to Damascus. Destroyed by grief, Rumi fell sick and asked his son, Sultan Valad, to go to Syria and bring Shams back. Shams returned, and with his return, the jealousy and hatred of the disciples boiled over again and became more threatening. On the evening of December 3, 1244, Shams and Rumi were sitting together in Rumi's house. There was a knock at the door. Shams got up calmly and said, "It is time; I am going. I am called to my death." He went out into the night and was never seen again. He was probably murdered by a group of disciples led by Rumi's oldest son. Rumi may not have found this out until many years later. He broke with all convention by not going to the funeral of his own son when he died.

At the time, however, Rumi clearly knew nothing of what had happened. For years, he persisted in believing that his beloved must still be alive. Twice, in an agony of longing and grief, he went to Damascus to try and find Shams, astounding and moving everyone by the tragic eloquence of his mourning and of the mystical ecstatic poems that now gushed from him. Rumi had been a dry and arrogant scholar. Rapture and anguish now made him the greatest of all mystic poets. Here are excerpts from what is perhaps the most beautiful, painful, and ecstatic of all the mystical love poems Rumi created for Shams after his "disappearance" or death:

In the end, you left, you went to the invisible,
O miracle of miracles! By what path
Did you escape from this world-prison?
You flapped your wings fiercely, and, shattering
  your cage
You took your flight and soared to the world of
  the soul.
You were a noble hawk, trapped in an old hag's shack.
When you heard the drum rattle, you left all space
  behind.
You were a drunken nightingale, trapped among owls.
The rose garden is perfume streamed towards you,
  you ran towards it.

*How exhausted you were by this harsh and bitter
    world—*
In the end, you left for the tavern of eternity.
You sped like an arrow to the target of pure joy . . .
This world, like a ghost, only gave you false signs.
You left all signs behind and ran to the signless.
*Since you have become the sun, what use would a
    crown be to you?*
Flowers flee autumn, but you, strangest of flowers,
As you faded, ran into the heart of the autumn wind!
You fell from heaven like rain on the roof of this earth.
You ran in every direction and left us a ladder of light...

It was on his second visit to Damascus that the final
mystery of Sham's and Rumi's mystical love affair
started to unfold in him. This is how his younger son,
Sultan Valad, describes what happened to his father
in those days.

> *He did not see Shams of Tabriz in Syria. He saw
> him in himself, clear as the moon. He said,
> "Although I am far from him physically without
> body or soul, we are one single light. If you want
> to, you can see him. If you want to, you can see
> me. I am him, He is me, O seeker! Both of us were
> together, without body and soul. Before this heavenly
> sphere began to turn, then there was no sphere, or
> moon or sun at all. Shams my beloved was for me
> like the soul. Before every heaven existed, we were
> abandoned to joy."*

There is nothing comparable to the passion, glory, and power of these amazing words of Rumi in any of the world's mystical traditions. Through the most terrible and wonderful of alchemies. Rumi's love for Shams and Shams' love for him had taken the man once known as Jalal-ud-Din to the highest peaks of divine love. Through loving the Eternal Beloved in Shams, Rumi had been transformed into love itself. Divine love had first annihilated him and then resurrected him in itself, as one of its faces in time.

In the three overwhelmingly intense and extreme years that he spent with Shams, Rumi was taken—dragged, perhaps, would be a better word—through nearly all the stages of the journey to unity with God. One last block or veil between Rumi and the Divine remained—the living and adored form of Shams himself.

Just as the full force of the spiritual power and presence of Jesus could not arrive to his disciples until after his crucifixion, resurrection, and ascension, the complete illumination of human and divine identity-in-love could not be unfolded in Rumi until after Shams' death, and Rumi's increasingly clear awareness of Shams living beyond death within him. The "form" of Shams was removed. The divine truth now arrived within Rumi to break him utterly and finally open, and to inspire him to all the great mystic masterpieces that have ensured him his highest of ranks among the world visionaries.

As Rumi himself had written:

There is no salvation for the soul
But to fall in love. . .
Only lovers can escape
From these two worlds.
This was written in creation.
Only from the heart
Can you reach the sky
The rose of Glory
Can only be grown in the heart.

For the next thirty years of his life, Rumi lived as an enlightened being, pouring out a wealth of teachings, poetry, and miracles. During these years, he wrote six books, 70,000 lines of a mystical epic, the "Mathnawi," that many religious Muslims consider the equal of the Koran. He founded the Mevlevi—or Mawlawiya—order that was later led and organized in depth by his son Sultan Valad.

The most famous ritual of this order is the "Sama," in which the sacred dance of the dervishes is performed. The cosmic dance was originated by the Master 700 years ago. "Many roads lead to God; I've chosen the one of dance and music."

The dance of the dervishes symbolizes the dance, the revolving of the planets, and everything that moves in the universe. In it, the whole cosmos reveals the divine joy that is manifesting it at every moment.

One afternoon, a few months before Rumi's death, a student found him listening to a flute player:

"Master, the afternoon prayer has just begun." Rumi turned to the young man and said calmly, "Listen to the music, because this is also the afternoon prayer."

What kind of person then was this enlightened Rumi? Many stories about Rumi echo the "fiorettis" of Francis of Assisi, his near contemporary, and show Rumi to have become in his final years a complete sage with a tender command of the whole animal order.

One day, Rumi was teaching near a pond where frogs were croaking noisily. He became annoyed and shouted, "What's all that noise about? Is it up to you to talk or to me?" At that moment, the frogs shut up and hopped onto the bank to listen to his teachings. When he had finished, he made a sign and they began croaking again.

Aflaki, Rumi's biographer, tells this story:

> One day, our Master stopped in the marketplace. All the inhabitants of the town were present. The Master turned his face from the people toward a wall, while continuing to teach mystical precepts. At the moment of the evening prayer, when night fell, the dogs of the marketplace formed a circle around him. He threw them loving and holy looks and continued his explanations. The dogs shook their heads and tails, moaning gently in rapture. Rumi said, "I swear by God that these dogs understand our gnosis. This door and this wall too proclaim the praises of God and understand the divine mysteries.

It wasn't only to animals, of course, that Rumi revealed the depths and richness and tender honesty of his enlightened self. He was loved by all the different classes of his world, by rulers and merchants and poor artisans alike, by people of all religious persuasions, by men and also by women, who found in him a champion of their dignity ahead of his time. He was a devoted friend, teacher, husband, and father. Few beings, if any, have lived a more completely or gloriously integrated life. Rumi exemplifies, in fact, the highest Sufi mystical ideal as expressed by Abu Sa'id in the eighth century: "The perfect mystic is not an ecstatic devotee lost in contemplation of oneness, nor a saintly recluse shunning all commerce with humanity. But the true saint goes in and out amongst the people and eats and sleeps with them and buys and sells in the market and takes part in social intercourse and never forgets God for a single moment."

In another lovely anecdote that perfectly expresses Rumi's enlightened tenderness, Aflaki tells us how one day Rumi, carrying a tray, was followed secretly by one of his disciples out of Konya. The disciple was bemused, because the tray was heaped with delicacies and Rumi himself always seemed to live austerely. Was the master a hypocrite? Did he plan to eat everything on the tray secretly somewhere? In fact, as the disciple discovered, Rumi was taking the food to a dog who had just given birth to six puppies in the ruins of an old house. Clearly Rumi's mystically awake senses had made him aware of the dog! When he saw his disciple, Rumi remarked, "You will know your heart is awake when you can hear a mother dog's soft cries of help from miles away."

The final teaching of a great Sage is in the way he or she dies. Rumi died with a sublime peacefulness and confidence. In the autumnal days of 1273, Rumi started to fade away. Physicians found water in his side, but could not diagnose why he was so weak. When a friend came to visit him in his last illness and was praying for his recovery, Rumi recited:

Why should I be unhappy
Because each parcel of my being is in full bloom?
Why should I not leave this pit?
Haven't I got a solid rope?
I constructed a pigeon house for the pigeons of the soul
Oh, Bird of my soul, fly away now
For I possess a hundred fortified towers.

Another friend asked him if he was afraid. Rumi smiled and pointed to his nightshirt, "When only this remains between lovers and beloved, how can I be afraid?"

Earthquakes shook Anatolia as he lay on his deathbed. On December 17, 1273, at sunset, with the sky turned red and flaming, as if to welcome his sacred heart, Rumi left his body and flew at last into the Sun of the Beloved. To this day, Sufis celebrate this as "Sheb-el-Arrus," Rumi's "wedding night."

The whole of his world, the whole of Konya, mourned him as a saint, a prophet, a sign of love that transcended all religious dogmas and divisions. Aflaki describes the outpouring of universal grief and spiritual tribute at Rumi's funeral:

After they had brought the corpse on a stretcher, all of the people, rich and poor alike, uncovered their heads. . . There was such an uproar you might have imagined that it was the day of resurrection. Everyone was crying and most of the men were wailing, tearing their robes, their bodies bare. Themembers of all communities and cultures were present: Christians, Jews, Greeks, Arabs, Turks. They were walking in front, each holding high their holybook. Each was reading the psalms, the Pentateuch, or the gospel, according to their faith. So great was the jostling and lamenting that the Muslims could not restrain them with canes or swords. The wild thunderous tumult was soon heard by the Sultan and his Emir Perwane, who sent for the leaders of these denominations and asked them why they were deeply moved when the one they were mourning was the"imam" of the Muslims. They answered, "When we saw Rumi, we understood the real nature of Christ, of Moses, and of all the other prophets. We have found, in him, the perfect conduct described in our books as being the conduct of the perfect prophets. Just as you Muslims claim that Rumi was the Mohammed of our time, so we think that he is the Moses and Jesus of our time, and just as you are his faithful friends, so are we, and a thousand timesmore, his servants and disciples. Did Rumi not say, 'Seventy-two sects will hear from us their own mystery. We are like a flute which, with a single node, is

tuned to two hundred religions?' Our master is the
sun of the truth which has shone on all human beings
and given them his favors. Everyone loves the sun
which lights up everyone's house.'"

Rumi is that sun. He could not have a truer epitaph.

I remember attending a business meeting in the offices of the distributors of Andrew Harvey's and my book, *Light upon Light*. Many of the people present were worried about obtaining permission from the author for the new translation! It did not occur to any of them, as Rumi was so vividly popular, that he had been dead for 700 years. But then, as Rumi wrote:

I have died time and time again,
And Your breath has revived me.
How can I die in dispersion before Your gatheredness?
Like the child that dies at his mother's breast,
I will die at the breast
Of the mercy and the bounty of the All-Merciful
What talk is this? How could the lover ever die?

The "deathless lover" in Rumi continues to speak directly to the "deathless lover" in us; and will do so as long as the soul has ears.

PART II

WAYS OF WORKING
WITH THE RUMI DECK

A VERY BRIEF HISTORY OF DIVINATION CARDS

Take the eyes of the one who sees as guide. —Rumi

To make this Rumi deck as authentic as possible, I wanted to inspire myself from the whole tradition of divination. Little did I begin to imagine how bizarre and colorful it would prove! As I dived deeper into it, what I discovered amazed, amused, and heartened me.

I discovered that the entire tradition of divination was, especially in its modern manifestations, an essentially anarchic and democratic one. At every turn, it affronted the official (and often all-controlling) powers of Church and State to try to empower people of all kinds in the heart of their lives. This is exactly what I want to do with the Rumi deck—to give people a holy but simple and direct tool to connect with their own divining powers and with the divine powers that rule Fate, so they can grow more confident and free.

I have come to think then of this Rumi deck as the latest and most sacred flowering of a great tree with many odd and twisted branches, the golden flower of the bizarre tree of divination, opening now, especially for us, and in a dangerous and thrilling time, when we need all the inspiration and guidance we can get.

Rumi, in his work, drew on folktales, popular songs, and sometimes scandalous anecdotes, transforming them all by his sacred wisdom. In the same way, I hope the Rumi deck transforms its origins through the power of Rumi's sacred knowledge. In other words, I hope the Rumi deck transforms an often erratic, dubious, and eccentric tradition and consummates something that always pervaded it in one way or another: the desire to help, inspire, and free human beings to be their full inventive, fearless, creative, and hopeful selves in all storms and situations.

The nineteenth-century author Court de Gebelin wrote a still very interesting history of divination. According to his sources, the first trace of divination through "cards," or through a collection of symbols picked at random by the consultant, can be found in Ancient Egypt (where else?).

In his time, Gebelin was the first to affirm that most of the symbols of the traditional Tarot decks (the Pope, the Empress, the Fool, etc...) were inspired by the great Egyptian mythological epic *The Book of Thot*.

In it, like Orpheus, Thot, father of Isis (the wife of Osiris, the Sun-God) went down into Hell to save his prisoner daughter and resurrect his murdered son-in-law. The story's main archetype is resurrection or, in other words, giving back life and restoring faith and hope. Gebelin goes far enough to unveil the etymology of the word "Tarot," which comes from the Egyptian "Ta" (way) and "Ro" (royal).

After the Ptolemeic period, the Romans brought back many Egyptian traditions with them, including some divination tools to add to the ones they were already using, such as studying the flight of the birds, the shape of the clouds, or the entrails of sacrificed animals.

It is likely that the divination cards remained in Italy until the country was attached to Germany with the establishment of the Holy Roman Empire in 800 AD. From then on, the game would spread in the counties of Provence—which included Avignon, the Papal capital of the epoch.

Fascinating the people and irritating the clergy, the practice of divination slowly became considered witchcraft and punishable by death. (One of the crimes of Victor Hugo's Esmeralda is divination.)

Another theory about the origins of divination cards has it that they were born in India, or somewhere in the Far East, and brought back to Europe by the Gypsies. The origins of the Gypsies are still controversial. Some claim they were nomads from a low Hindu cast that were chased from their land by the Islamic conqueror Tamburlaine. Experts in divination and witchcraft, they crossed the desert plains of India, Afghanistan, and Persia and then entered the Middle East through the Persian Gulf. There, they encountered the Crusaders and followed them back to Europe.

Other scholars maintain that divination cards were already introduced in Europe long before the arrival of the Gypsies and that to attribute to them the invention of Tarot reading (at that time, a form of witchcraft, don't forget) is one more form of racism toward them.

The occultist Eliphas Levi had yet another theory. He believed the cards came from the Hebrew tradition. According to him, they were invented by Enoch, son of Cain, and formed the basis of every sacred book of Antiquity. The original Tarot deck had, he claimed, been burned in the destruction of the Temple in the first century AD. Eliphas Levi, even if we cannot doubt his good will, belonged to an era that also contained Helena Blavatsky, Aleister Crowley, and the young Gurdjieff—an era that was in love with the exotic Occult and not too shy of hoaxes. Some similarities can be seen between Tarot and Kabbalah, but one must be extremely cautious about claiming the "Hebrew" origins of the Tarot.

Whatever their origins, the reading of divination cards continued throughout the late Middle Ages and the Renaissance. Some hand-painted Renaissance decks are pure masterpieces.

In the early eighteenth century, at the end of the 400-years craze of witch hunting, card reading again became legal. In the late 1700s, the Tarot would receive an extraordinary new infusion of life from a relative unknown supposedly called "Mademoiselle Lenormand."

Lenormand's sensational self-orchestrated fame gave a face-lift to the thousand-year-old deck. She claimed she could fly like a bird, and that she had escaped the guillotine by a whisker; but no records were ever found, of course. Rumor has it that "Mademoiselle" was a third-rate "Madam" trying to make ends meet. One day, she read the cards for a young woman who came from minor nobility and whose presumed drops of black blood—she was from Martinique—forbade her to dream of any social aspirations in "le tout Paris." The cards revealed that the young woman was to marry an ambitious man who would conquer Europe and that she would become Empress of France.

As with modern "gurus," having a rich, powerful, and famous patron helped a lot. Before long, through the patronage of Her Imperial Majesty Josephine, Empress of the French, Mademoiselle Lenormand became the toast of Paris. After the reestablishment of the "Ancient Regime" and the defeat of Waterloo, Mademoiselle Lenormand vanished from history, leaving her name to a Tarot deck, probably designed long after her death. Her gravestone in Paris' Pere Lachaise Cemetery, not far from Colette's and Jim Morrison's, is difficult to read, and voodoo knickknacks are often found there. So are pink carnations, the flowers of unrequited lovers. Mademoiselle Lenormand is now also known as a heavenly matchmaker.

The nineteenth century was a golden age for card-reading, but in a superficial way. Tarot, tea-leaf oracle, the use of crystal balls, etc. were a very Victorian hobby, but that did not often go much further than bridge or potpourri making.

Spirituality became very fashionable. The sisters Fox, in upstate New York, invented "modern spiritism," talking through a coffee-table with a spirit. In France, Hipolyte Rivail, a Lyon silk-maker, was, also through table tapping, instructed by a Druid who told him to exchange his name for a real Celtic one. (History repeats itself; nowadays, "channelers" are often instructed—or instruct others—to change their names to some Sanskrit pseudonym.) Hippolyte Rivail—now Allan Kardec—would become "The Pope of Spiritism." He left some pretty boring books and an ever-growing cult. His grave—also at the Pere Lachaise Cemetery, a "megalith-shaped" noblesse oblige for a Druid, is one of Paris' most visited "underground" sites.

Before she died, the one surviving Fox sister would confess in her old age that "it had all been jokes."

The two wars of the twentieth century would awaken a need for guidance and reassurance. So many mothers and fiancées would be anxious about the fate of a loved one on a battlefield somewhere in the East of France or the Lybian desert.

"Surrealists" and "dadaists" would sing the praises of Tarot reading, still sufficiently taboo not to be "recuperated" by the "Movement." The feverish Cocteau would write, "The Gypsy knew in advance our two lives would be seared by the winds," while Josephine Baker would triumph for nearly 50 years singing "Donnez-moi la main, je vais tout vous dire" (Let me read your palm; I'll tell you everything) all around the world. Today's television programs are regularly interrupted—often for the better—by ads for "psychic readings" of all kinds. Several Internet companies have also developed multimillion-dollar "psychic" projects.

Twenty-first-century borrowers, through Cyber-space, will be seeking for hope and light the same way that *The Book of Thot* readers did thousands of years ago.

Come to this deck with an open soul and leave what you call your "reason" behind, remembering Rumi's words:

Discursive reason's a vulture, my poor friend:
Its wings beat above a decaying corpse.
The Saint's reason is like the wings of Gabriel;
It soars in splendor, from stage to stage,
To rest in the shade of the Tree of Heaven.
It says, "I am a royal hawk, I am glorious and abundant,
I've nothing to do with a corpse, I'm not a vulture.
Leave the vulture behind and let me be your guide
Just one of my wings will be of more help to you
Than a hundred thousand vultures in full flight.

POLISHING THE HEART

Everyone I know has different and personal ways of preparing themselves to receive the divine guidance. One friend I know bathes and puts on fresh clothes before consulting the runes or throwing the I-Ching. Another fasts for two days, concentrating, at intervals, on the question or questions she wants helpful answers to. Another takes whatever "oracle" he wishes to use out on a trek with him into the mountains or the desert and once there, fasts, prays, and again and again begs for true help before he consults the oracle he has chosen.

Generally speaking, the more seriously and concentratedly you can prepare and purify your being, the more likely you are to receive clearly the instructions the divine is trying to send you, or the words of warning or encouragement. As Rumi wrote: "Still my being, o beloved, make it still as a mirror so your brilliant face can appear in it without stain."

The essential importance of "polishing the mirror of the heart" to the spiritual life in general and to the successful reception of divine guidance in particular is beautifully illustrated by a story Rumi tells in the *Mathnawi*, the story of the argument between the Byzantines and the Chinese on the art of painting and making portraits.

Both the Chinese and Byzantine schools of painters claimed to be the best, the most refined, and the most masterly. The Sultan decided to put them to the test.

The Chinese painters said, "Let us have one full room for us and another room for our rivals. Then we'll see who's best."

There were two rooms whose doors faced each other. The Chinese took one, the Byzantines the other. The Chinese asked the king to give them a hundred colors. The king opened his treasure chests and let them take all they wanted and saw to it that his treasures supplied them with everything they needed. The Byzantines declared, however, "We don't need color and we don't need paint. All we need to do is to remove the dirt." They shut their doors and started to polish the walls until they became pure and brilliant like a cloudless spring day.

When the Chinese had finished their work, they were ecstatic and started to beat drums. The King came in and saw what they had painted and was delighted. Then he went to where the Byzantines were. The curtain separating the two rooms was drawn back. There, on walls pure of any stain, appeared the reflection of the Chinese paintings. Everything that had amazed the Sultan in the other room seemed even more wonderful here. He wept with wonder.

The Byzantines, Rumi tells us, are the mystics who "have polished their hearts and washed them pure of desire, greed, avarice, and hate." And as Rumi says of the heart, "All these worlds and dimensions are numbered and limited. The mirror of the heart is limitless. Here, all understanding falls silent if it doesn't want to betray, for the heart is with God, or, rather, the heart is God."

To reflect reality truly and to receive accurately the guidance of the divine at all moments we need to keep the "mirror" of the heart "polished." As Rumi informs us, "Polish your heart and you'll soar above all color and perfume. You will contemplate beauty ceaselessly from heaven. . . You will receive, continuously, hundreds of impressions. Why do I say impressions? I mean: the direct vision of God."

Over the years of developing and experimenting with *The Rumi Deck*, I have evolved three simple methods of polishing my heart mirror, which I would like to share with you:

- polishing the heart with a name of God,
- polishing the heart with a prayer,
- polishing the heart with devoted silence.

These three methods can, if you want, be combined into one continuous method in three parts. Any combination of them can be used in any order. Be creative and see for yourself what works best for you.

Here, then, are three simple and powerful exercises that can help you "polish your heart" and still your mind so you can "hear" what God is trying to tell you through the cards of the Rumi deck.

EXERCISE 1: POLISHING THE HEART WITH A NAME OF GOD

Begin by sitting quietly, with a straight back, breathing deeply and calmly. Allow your mind slowly to empty of thought. Now begin to say out loud, but softly and reverently, the name of God that you most love. If you are a Christian this could be Jesus or Mary; if you are a Hindu you might use "Krishna" here; if you are a Muslim you will probably say "Allah." If you do not practice any particular religion, use whatever name or phrase for God most moves you.

Just keep on saying the name, again and again, softly and reverently, for about ten minutes, focusing your whole attention in your spiritual heart-center, which is situated to the right of your physical heart in the middle of your chest.

Imagine that each time you say the name of God you have chosen, the shadowed mirror of your heart becomes brighter and brighter, until at the end of the practice, it is a pool of softly burning light.

Now, you are ready to receive the wisdom of the cards. As you start to consult them, pray to the divine to be guided.

EXERCISE 2: POLISHING THE HEART WITH A PRAYER

Some people find it hard just to repeat the name of God in the heart. For them, it is easier to use a prayer. The prayer I find most useful is one that is very holy to all Muslims, since it was created by the prophet Muhammed. It is a prayer that anyone can use, because its wording and message are universal.

The prayer goes as follows:

Oh God, give me light in my heart and light in my tongue and light in my hearing and light in my see-ing and light in my feeling and light in every part of my body and light before me and light behind me. Give me, I beg you, light on my right hand and light on my left hand and light above me and light beneath me. O Lord, make light grow within me and give me light and illuminate me.

As you pray this magnificent prayer, imagine that your whole being, from the crown of your head to the bottom of your feet, becomes increasingly filled with divine light. Repeat the prayer, slowly in your heart-center, out loud or inwardly. Imagine everything you ask for, and offer up each part of your body and being as you name it. Continue the repetition, peacefully, for about ten min-utes. Now you are ready, because you have asked to be illuminated by divine love and wisdom. To receive divine guidance from the cards, pray to be open to what they will say, and pray for what you are asking for and what you need in your own words.

EXERCISE 3: POLISHING THE HEART WITH DEVOTED SILENCE

Sit quietly and retreat inwardly into the purest, most silent and tender part of your heart, the part that mystics of all traditions tell us is always turned in intimate adoration towards the divine.

Without using words, allow the longing of your heart to grow inside you and become more intense and passionate. Sometimes, to awaken this wordless longing, it is helpful to put both hands on the heart-center, bow your head, and repeat "Beloved, beloved, beloved," with all the fervor of your being. When the love inside you is aware, stop saying the word. Become one with the love you are, and let it flow and expand.

Now imagine that your longing for God has summoned the divine as a sea of sweet fire in which your entire being and everything around you is plunged, from the crown of your head to the tips of your toes. Every single cell in your body is saturated with this sweet fire. Even the small hairs on your arms and legs burn in it.

Inevitably, thoughts and emotions will arrive. Imagine that as you "see" them "coming," you stretch out an imaginary arm, seize them by the neck, and drown them in the sea of fire around you and in you. Slowly, you should feel a dynamic, intense silence growing in your being and mind. This dynamic silence is the pure force of divine love working directly within you.

This is a very powerful and holy exercise, so you should practice it with great sincerity. Continue with it for at least ten minutes, so that its effects can be felt and its purifying and clarifying power are allowed to work.

Now you are ready to hear what the divine is trying to say to you through the cards. Pray for guidance and for what you need.

Hear from the heart wordless mysteries!
Understand what cannot be understood!
In man's stone-dark heart there burns a fire
That chars all veils to their root and foundation.
When the veils are burned away, the heart will
understand completely.
Ancient love will unfold ever-fresh forms
In the heart of the spirit, in the core of the heart.

May all our hearts become so "polished" by sincere love of and trust in God, so that we can always be receptive to "ancient love's ever-fresh forms."

May the cards of the Rumi deck speak to you with the voice of love!

METHODS OF READING AND SOME ADVICE

Once you have polished your heart—or prepared yourself—you are ready to use the cards. Part III of this book can help you determine what any given card might mean in your life now. The cards are divided into families, which indicate general areas of importance or concern. The layouts presented here are adaptations of traditional ways of interpreting cards. The methods that I am giving here are only suggestions. Rumi said, "The door and the wall tell subtle things; Fire, Water and Earth are storytellers."

My first advice would be to tell you, "Listen to your inner guidance" and invent methods of your own.

One very helpful and inspiring way for me to use the cards—especially if you are, like most of us, busy, overwhelmed by the pressure of daily life, and need direct help—is the simplest one of all. Just concentrate a few minutes on the object of your question. Be always sure that you are formulating your request for guidance in the simplest way. Just concentrate and select one card as the meditation for the day.

Find a place in your home—on your desk, perhaps, or on the kitchen table?—where you'll read the cards often, or carry them in your pocket: Allow the message to keep on *reaching you*.

THE SIMPLE SPREAD

This method is strongly advised for "minor" problems, if there are such things.

1   What brought up the present situation?
2   The present situation.
3   The future, and how to deal with it.

THE CELTIC CROSS

The cards should be turned face up from 6 to 1, with 1 being the last card to be read.

1   This card represents what's for the person who is laying out the cards.

2   This represents what's against the situation.

3   The present. What's going on now.

4   The recent past.

5   The distant past.

6   The future.

THE CLOCK METHOD

This method of reading is more complex than the previous ones. It is directly inspired by a Runic method and gives a very detailed view of the current situation, how to deal with it, and where it is leading. This method is invaluable for getting the large picture in a temporal or spiritual difficulty, but should be used sparingly and prepared for in a sacred atmosphere. I advise you to meditate and pray for at least twenty minutes before using this method, so you can approach the reading in as calm and open a way as possible.

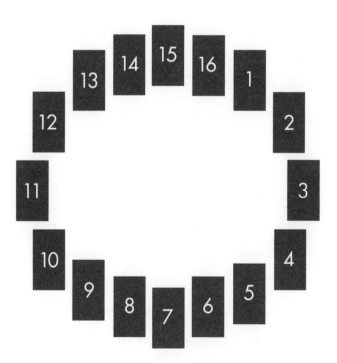

1 & 2   The first two cards indicate how the consultants can use the message to solve whatever problem they are asking about. These are the cards of personal power, and indicate to consultants on what resources they are to draw.

3 & 4   These cards show the state of the consultant's spiritual or mental being. They can be a health warning or warnings of close danger, and should always be taken soberly.

5 & 6   These cards represent the past and what brought the consultants to where they find themselves. They help uncover the hidden roots of present situations and to give the consultant essential information for going forward.

7 & 8   These cards need to be studied carefully. They represent the obstacles that block the consultant's path. They could be considered the axis of the spread.

9 & 10   These cards unveil the origins of the obstacles ahead and can frequently point to the people involved in them.

11 & 12	These cards show what is happening in the present and what today's situation is and promises.
13 & 14	These cards represent the immediate future and what is waiting to be born out of the present situation.
15 & 16	The two final cards deal with the likely outcome if all the different forms of advice given in the spread are followed.

After you have finished your reading, pray for what you need and want and offer up thanks to Rumi and to God for the help you have been given. This is extremely important because praise and thanksgiving will help Divine Grace reach you faster.

When you have really digested the meaning of the reading, write it down as clearly and fully as possible on a piece of paper so you can consult it to refresh your memory or your resolution when you need to.

As I said at the beginning, use this large "Clock Method" sparingly. It is a great mistake to consult oracles too often. It only leads to confusion. Trust the method, prepare yourself deeply to receive its guidance and follow the guidance, you receive with sincerity.

May this sublime poem by Rumi inspire your journey:

WATERS CONSTANTLY FLOWING

This entire world's the form of Universal Reason,
Which is the Father of all lovers of the Divine World
Be ungrateful towards Him and nothing can change.
Make your peace with your Father, abandon
    disobedience,
And this world's water and clay will appear like a
    gold carpet
And Resurrection become your immediate experience
And heaven and earth be transfigured in your eyes.
Since I'm always at peace with my Father,
The world always appears like a paradise to me.
At each moment, a new form and new beauty appear
And their glory dissolves all fear and boredom.
I see the world radiant and brimming with
    magnificence;
The waters constantly flowing from the Spring
    of Heaven.
The sound of these waters is always enchanting
    my ears;
My deepest mind and conciousness reel with bliss.
The branches of the trees dance for me like penitents;
I see leaves everywhere clapping their hands
    like musicians.
The mirror's shining seeps through its velvet sheath—
Imagine the blaze when the Mirror itself appears!

PART III

THE RUMI CARDS

THE FAMILIES

Through reading Rumi again and again and meditating on the different aspects, stages, and revelations of the path to God that he lived and described, I gradually came to understand that the most helpful way of presenting his mystical guidance would be to divide it into different families. Each one would reflect a different facet of the diamond of the Path and would represent that facet of Divine guidance that the Path is turning to the Seeker.

The Rumi deck includes six families: Birth, Love, Ordeal, Transformation, Warnings, and Rewards. In all, there are fifty-four cards, nine in each family. The families are color-keyed on the cards as follows: saffron equals birth, Tibetan red equals love, eggplant equals ordeal, prussian blue equals transformation, persimmon equals warnings, evergreen equals rewards.

THE BIRTH CARDS

Each moment of our lives is potentially a new birth, if our hearts are open. Rumi always claimed that the wind of grace is always blowing from God, but that we are too rarely open to its fertile power. Nevertheless, through Divine generosity, signs of new birth constantly dance in and out of our lives, inviting us to hope, creativity, passion, and praise!

This family then, is dedicated to these signs, to good omens, to mysterious indications of awakening, of new blood, and to the healing flow of new possibilities. In other words, we celebrate here all forms of that birthing power that floods life with divine beauty and glory.

The birth cards serve to remind us all of the possibilities we ignore, that are always struggling to flower in us.

Meditate on each of them and some of the perfume of the heart of Rumi will freshen your whole spirit.

Love has come to rule and transform;
Stay awake, my heart, stay awake.

> *Be accutely aware of*
> *the hidden teachings and*
> *blessings you are about*
> *to receive.*

The fragrance, my friend, that floats to you this moment
streams from the tent of the secrets of God.

> *Your life has reached a*
> *decisive and very positive*
> *turning point.*

The world grows green again, and runs with gardens.
Jewels from the mines glitter in each tree;
Souls open like suns and link with one another.

> *Harmony and prosperity*
> *join hands in your life:*
> *Be grateful.*

Happiness is more precious than wealth;
May millions of mercies rain on your dancing!

*You have chosen inner
joy and not power in the
world. This is why God
is blessing you.*

They offered many reasons
Why the rose is laughing
None of them knew the truth:
Its prayer has been granted by Spring.

*The true reason for the
joy you feel is that it
comes from Divine grace.*

Look for the soul, you become soul;
Hunt for the bread, you become bread;
Whatever you look for, you are.

*Be careful: What you
choose could determine
what you become.*

Your soul was a snake, but is now a fish;
It leaps in the spring of immortal life.

*Love and hard work have
changed you from some-
one who was struggling
into someone who lives
in joy.*

You touched the egg of my heart:
It broke apart.
The bird of heaven is opening its wings.

*Inspirations of all kinds
flood your mind: Seize
the time.*

Open your eyes and you will see at last He is walking in
your garden like the breeze at dawn.

*Have the courage to
count your blessings and
you will find hidden
resources.*

THE LOVE CARDS

Rumi wrote, "Wherever you may be, in whatever situation or circumstance you may find yourself, strive always to be a lover, and a passionate lover. Once you possess you heart in love, you will always be a lover, in the tomb, at the Resurrection, and in paradise forever and ever."

He also wrote, "Adore Him and love Him with your whole being, and he will reveal to you that each thing in the universe is a vessel full to the brim with wisdom and beauty."

For Rumi—as for all those who have seen the truth—love is the One Supreme Power, and to know and live in love is the only reason for being here.

Love reveals its blinding glory only to those prepared to give everything for it—and only to those willing and able to surrender to its laws.

Rumi constantly, and with an unmatched eloquence and passion, reminds us that a life without love is not a life at all, and that only love will speak for anyone of us "at the Day of Resurrection."

As he says in one of his most beautiful odes, "All that we will take across the waters of Death is the jewel of love."

The family of love cards, then, refers to and celebrates love in all its holy forms. The love between friends, lovers, families, and spiritual seekers.

Nothing is more important than to inspire ourselves continually with the beauty of love that the mystics glimpse. That gives us the courage to live authentic, honest, and passionate lives and to refuse the seductions of the world.

Love, of course, can also be painful and involves subtle forms of death. Rumi, of all people, knew the price of love, and knew, too, the ecstasy and sublime rapture that such death can prepare.

THE POETRY AND KEYS OF THE LOVE CARDS

Each night, the Moon kisses secretly the lover who counts
the stars.

> *Pay constant attention*
> *to the Divine guidance*
> *and you will be blessed.*

Fall into his hands and you'll weep like clouds;
Run from him and you'll freeze over like snow.

> *You have to choose love*
> *knowing clearly its*
> *conditions!*

It is certain that an atom of goodness on the path of faith
is never lost.

> *Never lose faith that*
> *your acts of love go*
> *unnoticed. May also be*
> *an invitation to more*
> *generous actions.*

The horizons you've promised will be brilliant with signs;
I am sick of shadows; Blind me with you!

> *Your whole being cries*
> *out for a change that*
> *will come.*

Hold me in the fire; And although I die, I know for whom
and why.

> *Love has brought*
> *you to the moment*
> *when you can choose it*
> *without fear.*

You are the divine calendar where all destinies are written; The ocean of mercy where all faults are washed clean.

> *You understand clearly*
> *the nature of love: That*
> *it is the only way forward.*

Open your heart, and you will hear the lutes of the Angels.

Love establishes for you
a direct connection to
heaven, to the Divine.

Dive into the boiling sea of passion and all grief will run from you.

You have been suffering
because your heart was
cold. Now risk the fire
of love!

If it is love you are looking for, Take a knife and cut off the head of fear.

It is a time when love
itself is willing to teach
you the truth directly.
To find love, destroy
your old patterns.

THE ORDEAL CARDS

Rumi tells us that it was the custom in Qazwin for the men to have symbols tattooed on their bodies. A coward went to a tattoo artist and said "Now, please, tattoo a lion on my back." As soon as he felt the first prick of the needles he shouted, "What part of the lion are you doing now?" The tattooist replied, "The tail." "Forget the tail, do another part!" The tattooist started on another part of the lion. The man again began to yell and demand that he begin again somewhere else. Wherever the tattooist put his needles, the client screamed. Eventually, the tattooist became so angry that he flung his needles and colors on the floor and refused to go any further.

One of the glories of Rumi's work is its naked honesty about the necessity of ordeal—about what could be called "the alchemy of Agony."

As the story of the man and the tattooed lion shows, to have the right to wear the sign of the lion, the bravest and most majestic of animals, and so for the Sufis one of the holiest images of the Lover, you have to prove your courage, patience, acceptance, magnanimity, and surrender to the will of God.

How can virtues be proved except in the whirlwind of trouble? How can your "inner God" be tested except in the crucible of anguish?

The alchemy of Agony is not only, however, harsh or fierce. It is also the highest form of Divine Mercy—which many in the New Age have deliberately forgotten. We are in the hands of the Supreme Alchemist, and one of the holiest lessons Rumi has tried to teach us is that all the ordeals that are sent to us are sent for our transformation. And however terrible they may seem, they are guided by love.

This family of ordeal cards, then, deals with both sides of the nature of suffering in our lives: that it is unavoidable and that, through understanding its inner purpose, it can be transmuted into the gold of Grace.

You want everything to be yours?
Become nothing to yourself and all things.

> *The only hope to find a*
> *solution to the problem is*
> *through total detachment.*

Humanity is bewildered by false idols
And driven by vain fantasies into the pit of destruction.

> *Your illusions threaten*
> *everything you hold*
> *dear: Be aware. Danger*
> *is near.*

The rock of the truth is hard and inflexible. It doesn't fear
a world made of bits of broken brick.

> *Stand for what you*
> *really believe.*
> *Whatever happens.*

With this pain, You are digging a path for yourself.

> *The suffering you are*
> *undergoing will lead to*
> *true wisdom.*

From every direction, Agonies have crowded you; To drag
you at last toward the directionless.

> *The meaning of all the*
> *losses you are sustaining*
> *is to turn you totally*
> *toward the Divine.*

Before you pierce an abscess with a knife
How can it heal and how can you regain your health?

> *Your situation is agoniz-*
> *ing now but it will free*
> *you from what has been*
> *blocking you.*

You fear the rocks? Better men than you have died on them. Dying on love's rocks is better than a life of death.

Stop being afraid and full of self-pity. Your duty is to act on your deepest beliefs.

Don't despair if the friend sends you away; He may chase you away today; He'll call for you tomorrow.

Things look dark now, but will soon change completely, for the better Can also mean, don't judge a friend too hastily.

You'll only enjoy the City and your relations, After enduring all the griefs and ordeals of exile.

After all you have been through, joy and prosperity will taste even better.

THE TRANSFORMATION CARDS

In the universe of Love, all things are in perpetual
metamorphosis. Love powers an endless evolution
and a cosmic dance in which all things constantly are
born and die and change shape.

Excrement and dead leaves become compost for a
new birth. A protracted sorrow engenders dazzling
joy, new visions of an abundant knowledge dance in
the skull. This family of transformation cards celebrates both faces of the Moon of Transformation.
The shining one turned toward us in promise and
hope and mysterious invitation also has the dark face
that hints of strange rites of passage still to be
endured and skins still to be shed. It also, by implica-

tion, makes us aware that the Moon constantly turns from one to the other, and prepares us to be brave in difficulty and humble in fulfillment.

Respecting what could be called the "law of the Cosmic Dance of Transformation" is one of the most beautiful rewards of mystic understanding, and one of the signs of the union of the Lover with the Beloved.

As Rumi wrote:

One day, in your wine shop,
I drank a little wine,
And threw off the robe of this body
And knew, drunk on you,
This world is Harmony
Creation, Destruction—
I am dancing for them both.

May each of these cards bring you a taste of that wine and teach you a step in Love's eternal dance.

THE POETRY AND KEYS OF THE TRANSFORMATION CARDS

Gold becomes constantly more and more beautiful
From the blows the jeweler inflicts on it.

> *Realize that what you have found difficult is bringing you closer to your goal.*

Before death takes what has been given to you,
You must give away everything you can give.

> *Generosity is the key to*
> *everything you really*
> *want: Act now.*

How can victory be won without spiritual war and
patience? Give proof of patience; Faith is the key to joy.

> *Trust that a happy out-*
> *come is bound to come*
> *in time.*

Say with each breath "Make me humbler, make me humbler";
When you are small as an atom, you will know his glory.

> *The potential of the*
> *situation will be*
> *revealed only to humble*
> *minds and hearts.*

If you know how to be patient, He'll offer you the seat of honor; He'll show you a hidden way that no one will know.

> *Things seem impossible.*
> *Wait and trust and*
> *you will be shown the*
> *solution.*

How many years do you need for the ruby, through the Sun's work, to obtain its rich color and its dazzle?

> *Great projects and*
> *achievement require*
> *time and patience.*
> *Success will take time:*
> *but will come.*

Put your trust in him who gives Life and Ecstasy. Don't mourn what doesn't exist. Cling to what does.

> *Don't look back at the*
> *past. Turn your head to*
> *wisdom and truth.*

Anyone who asks to be illuminated now will be made
A torch to light up the World.

*This is a time radiant
with blessings: Realize
your deepest dreams.*

Through Love, disaster becomes good fortune.
Through love, a prison becomes a garden.

*The way from defeat to
victory runs through
love: Things are never as
bad as you imagine
them to be.*

THE WARNING CARDS

"I knew it!" How many times have we heard or said such a thing? The intelligence of Love tries constantly to protect us and to warn us, but we are vain and follow our desires and illusions, and so fill our lives with chaos and confusion.

One of the essential features of a real seeker's life is to start humbly listening to the warnings—inner and outer—that the universe will always be trying to give him or her. This takes true discrimination, what Jesus called "the wisdom of the Serpent," detachment from our own plans, and a constant willingness to listen to the often quiet and obvious instructions of the Divine.

This family of warnings, then, is intended to make us all as alert as possible to the shifting currents of Fate and to the hidden motivations of others, which, if we do not attend to them, can destroy us.

No warning is final. Fate always gives us hints before it strikes. If we learn the Art of Attention, then we do the best we can for ourselves to secure our growth.

Let's—one more time—listen to Rumi:

Attend to the warnings that will come,
Do not expose what you are and have to
  destruction,
Remember how frail you are,
Who are less than a straw.

THE POETRY AND KEYS OF THE WARNING CARDS

Support patiently the disagreements inflicted by ignorant men.

> *Fight against fools and*
> *you make matters worse:*
> *Keep calm.*

Don't go anywhere, I beg you;
The Moon you are looking for is inside you.

> *Realize that everything*
> *you need is where you are.*

Light the lamp, trim its wick and keep it filled with oil;
Don't say you'll act tomorrow, tomorrow;
Tomorrow's already gone.

> *Stop delaying: Act now*
> *or your plans will fail.*

Do not call a cup the Sea;
Do not call mad the sage of Love.

> *Do not inflate your*
> *experience: Honor the*
> *true wisdom.*

If a tree could only walk,
He would never have to fear being chopped down.

> *Keep always changing*
> *and growing.*

Are you dazed from too much meat and wine?
Or are you a soldier on the field of battle?

> *Look at what you are*
> *doing and decide if your*
> *motives are selfish or*
> *brave.*

The mirror of the heart must be polished constantly
Before you can see clearly in it Good and Evil.

*Do not rely on your
own judgment. Pray for
guidance.*

Whoever doesn't show himself humble today
Will tomorrow be humiliated like Pharaoh.

*Your pride is putting
you in danger. Choose
the path of humility.
Do not be fooled by
appearances.*

The carnal soul's food is seeds of evil;
Sow them and they grow and grow irresistibly.

*You are in danger of
making very bad choices
which will damage
your life.*

THE REWARD CARDS

The divine Love that urges our journey ever onward also constantly and lavishly rewards us for every sacrifice we make and every action of true generosity that we undertake.

Rumi tells a wonderful story about how the Queen of Sheba, when she visited King Solomon, wanted to impress him, and so brought with her 40 camels laden with gold. When she arrived in his kingdom, however, she saw that all the streets, even the humblest ones, were paved with gold. Solomon said to her, "I do not need any of your gifts. All I need from you is to be worthy of the million gifts I will shower upon you."

When the eyes of Love really open in us, we see that life is an unbroken stream of ordinary miracles and that just to be alive is a matchless reward. This family of rewards, then, celebrates the gold thread of blessings that runs through Life's red and black carpet and invites us always to keep our hearts in a state of adoration.

When Sheba saw how much the King loved her, an infinite love for him started to grow in her heart, and to lead her to the Palace of Eternal Wisdom.

May these cards be signs on the map to that Palace and may each one of them glint with the mystery of Solomon's gold!

THE POETRY AND KEYS OF THE REWARD CARDS

Eat on and on, you lovers, at Eternity's table;
Its feast is forever; And spread out for you.

> *Prosperity of all kinds is now open to you.*

Dawn; Its breezes swim with musk; Wake up!
Breathe in this fragrance!

> *A wonderful fresh beginning is inviting you to act: Be aware!*

If you read nothing and wisdom sees your fervor,
Awareness will sit in your hand like a tamed dove.

*What you need to know
will come to you if you
are humble. Look for
knowledge in your heart,
and not in the world.*

A swan beats its wings with joy;
"Rain, pour on!
God has lifted my soul from the water."

*A dark and difficult
period is now finally
over. Express your joy.*

He's here. Invisible. Absolute.
And he makes the world grow fragrant.

*The blessings you have
been looking for have at
last arrived.*

Let all candles gutter out!
The Moon is waiting to shine around.

*Leave all your small
projects. The big reward
you want is coming.*

After despair, many hopes flourish.
Just as after darkness, Thousands of Suns open and
Start to shine.

> *Your suffering has*
> *earned you a glorious*
> *fresh start.*

Your grief lasted so long ...
Look, healing is here.
Your door was locked.
Look, here is the key.

> *Just when you are about*
> *to give up hope, the*
> *solution becomes*
> *obvious.*

The more you strive to reach the place of Splendor,
The more the invisible Angels will help you.

> *God and destiny reward*
> *those who give every-*
> *thing. You could also see*
> *this card as a message*
> *from your Guardian*
> *Angel to connect with it.*

A FINAL MESSAGE

A few years ago, when I moved from the Bay Area to the Nevada desert, I surprised many of my friends, who simply could not believe that you could lead a "spiritual" life just ten miles away from the MGM Grand Hotel and Casino!

The desert is a strange place. When I walk in Red Rock Canyon at dusk, I always understand—or seem to, anyway—why the first fathers of the Church went into its dry solitude. There is no place left to hide in its harsh light; God is near.

Las Vegas is an ever-growing city. Still, every evening in the summer months the wind brings the perfume of the blooming sage bushes, which is even more rich when there's a storm brewing.

If you are ready to listen, God will talk to you wherever you are. There are no such things as "Sacred Places" or "Sacred States." Oh, yes, there are, and they are called "everywhere you are" and "daily life." You can receive life-changing guidance listening to Tina Turner, while some might wait for days sitting on a "vortex"(!) in Sedona.

Open your heart to this deck, let all your worries go, and ask for what you need with a child's soul. You will be answered. This is not a promise; this is a certainty.

Let us end as we started, with Rumi:

Who can describe the action of the matchless one?
Sometimes God's action is like this, sometimes
  quite different
The work of God is nothing but astonishment.

JOSEPH AND THE MIRROR

A friend of Joseph's came to visit him after returning
from a long journey. "What present have you brought
me?" Joseph asked. "What could I bring you," the
friend replied, "that you don't already have?" "But,"
he added, "because you are so beautiful, and nothing
exists in all the worlds more beautiful than you, I have
brought you a mirror, so you can know the joy at every
moment of seeing your own face."
Is there anything that God doesn't have already
that you could give Him? Is there anything that
God could need that you could possibly provide?
All you are here for, and the entire meaning of the
Path of Love, is to bring before God a heart bright
as a mirror, so God can see His own face in it.

FOR FURTHER EXPLORATION OF RUMI

If you want to deepen your knowledge of Rumi's life and work, here are some books that I have found moving and useful:

Arberry, A.J., *Discourses of Rumi*, London, John Murray, 1961.

Banks, Coleman, *The Essential Rumi*, San Francisco, Harper San Francisco, 1995.

Schimmel, AnneMarie, *I Am Wind, You Are Fire: The Life and Work of Rumi*, Boston, Massachusetts, Shambhala Publications, 1992.

—*The Triumphal Sun*, London, East West Publications, 1978.

Chittick, W.C., *The Sufi Path of Love: The Spiritual Teachings of Rumi*, Albany, New York, State University of New York Press, 1983.

Harvey, Andrew, *The Way of Passion: A Celebration of Rumi*, Berkeley, California, Frog Ltd, 1994.

—*The Teachings of Rumi,* Boston, Massachuesetts, Shambala Publications, 1999.

—*Love's Glory: Re-creation of Rumi*, Berkeley, California, Balthazar/North Atlantic, 1996.

Star, Jonathon and Shiva, Shahram, *A Garden Beyond Paradise: The Mystical Poetry of Rumi*, New York, Bantam Books, 1992.

Here are some audio sets that I have found helpful in my journey into Rumi and Sufism:

Barks, Coleman, *Rumi, Voice of Longing*, Sounds True Recordings, 1994.

Harvey, Andrew, *Rumi, The Song of the Sun*, Sounds True Recordings, 1999.

Vaughan-Lee, Llewellyn, *Love Is a Fire and I Am Wood, The Sufi's Mystical Journey Home*, Sounds True Recordings 1998.

Entering the Heart of Hearts: The Sufi Path of Love, Sounds True Recordings, 1999.

THE RUMI CARD BOOK
was produced by double-u-gee
in Petaluma, California. The book
and package were designed by
Michele Wetherbee. The typefaces
are BradloSlab, Futura, Sabon
and Trajan. Based on traditional
Islamic art, the illustrations were
drawn by Stefan Gutermuth.